WEEKLY **WR** READER®

EARLY LEARNING LIBRARY

My Day at School

After School

by Joanne Mattern

Reading consultant: Susan Nations, M.Ed.,
author/literacy coach/
consultant in literacy development

Please visit our web site at: www.garethstevens.com
For a free color catalog describing Weekly Reader® Early Learning Library's list
of high-quality books, call 1-877-445-5824 (USA) or 1-800-387-3178 (Canada).
Weekly Reader® Early Learning Library's fax: (414) 336-0164.

Library of Congress Cataloging-in-Publication Data

Mattern, Joanne, 1963-
After school / by Joanne Mattern.
p. cm. — (My day at school)
Includes bibliographical references and index.
ISBN-10: 0-8368-6783-1 — ISBN-13: 978-0-8368-6783-1 (lib. bdg.)
ISBN-10: 0-8368-6790-4 — ISBN-13: 978-0-8368-6790-9 (softcover)
1. School children—Juvenile literature. I. Title.
HQ781.M362 2006
372.18—dc22   2006005133

Copyright © 2007 by Weekly Reader® Early Learning Library

This edition first published in 2007 by
Weekly Reader® Early Learning Library
A Member of the WRC Media Family of Companies
330 West Olive Street, Suite 100
Milwaukee, WI 53212 USA

Editor: Barbara Kiely Miller
Art direction: Tammy West
Cover design and page layout: Kami Strunsee
Picture Research: Diane Laska-Swanke
Photographer: Gregg Andersen

Printed in the United States of America

1 2 3 4 5 6 7 8 9 10 09 08 07 06

amer. Kids Preview 10/06 14.95

Note to Educators and Parents

Reading is such an exciting adventure for young children! They are beginning to integrate their oral language skills with written language. To encourage children along the path to early literacy, books must be colorful, engaging, and interesting; they should invite the young reader to explore both the print and the pictures.

The *My Day at School* series is designed to help young readers review the routines and rules of a school day, while learning new vocabulary and strengthening their reading comprehension. In simple, easy-to-read language, each book follows a child through part of a typical school day.

Each book is specially designed to support the young reader in the reading process. The familiar topics are appealing to young children and invite them to read — and re-read — again and again. The full-color photographs and enhanced text further support the student during the reading process.

In addition to serving as wonderful picture books in schools, libraries, homes, and other places where children learn to love reading, these books are specifically intended to be read within an instructional guided reading group. This small group setting allows beginning readers to work with a fluent adult model as they make meaning from the text. After children develop fluency with the text and content, the book can be read independently. Children and adults alike will find these books supportive, engaging, and fun!

— Susan Nations, M.Ed., author, literacy coach, and consultant in literacy development

School is over. It is time
to go home.

5

I take the **school bus** home.

Mom is waiting for me.

I put my **backpack** on the table. I hang up my coat.

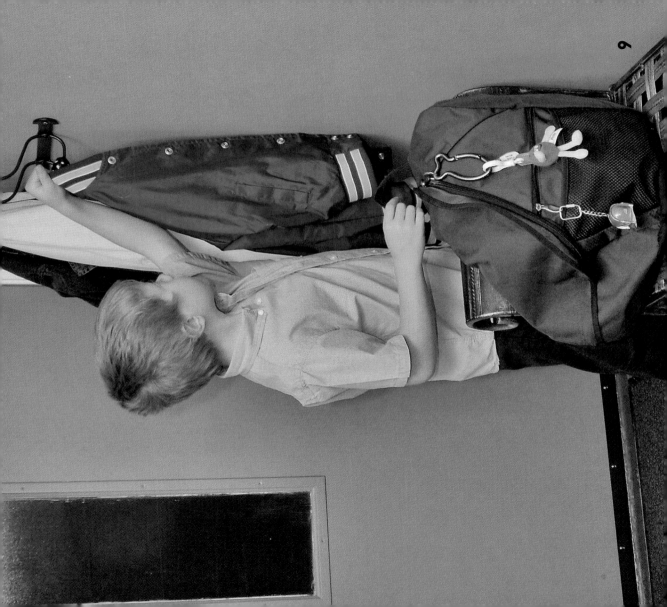

I am hungry. Mom makes
a snack for me.

11

Then I play outside.
I like to ride my bike.

Now it is time for my **karate lesson.** Mom drives me to the class.

I do my **homework** before dinner. Mom helps me sometimes.

I read a book after dinner.
I brought the book home
from school. Dad listens
to me read.

Then I watch TV with Dad.

Soon I will go to bed.

Tomorrow is a new day
at school!

Glossary

backpack — a bag worn on the back to carry books and supplies

homework — school work that is done at home

hungry — wanting food to eat

karate — a form of self-defense that uses kicks and punches

lesson — a class or happening that teaches something

school bus — a bus that students take to and from school

For More Information

Books

After School Stuff. Cara J. Stevens (Lowell House Juvenile)

Bike Riding. After-School Fun (series). JoAnn Early Macken (Gareth Stevens)

Karate. After-School Fun (series). JoAnn Early Macken (Gareth Stevens)

Web Site

Bike Tour

www.nhtsa.dot.gov/kids/biketour/index.html

Learn how to ride safely. This site features bike laws, information on bike equipment and helmets, and more.

Publisher's note to educators and parents: Our editors have carefully reviewed this Web site to ensure that it is suitable for children. Many Web sites change frequently, however, and we cannot guarantee that a site's future contents will continue to meet our high standards of quality and educational value. Be advised that children should be closely supervised whenever they access the Internet.

Index

About the Author

Joanne Mattern has written more than one hundred and fifty books for children. Joanne also works in her local library. She lives in New York State with her husband, three daughters, and assorted pets. She enjoys animals, music, going to baseball games, reading, and visiting schools to talk about her books.